My German name is

____

My English name is

____

My photo

2 Hobbies

My hobby is

Monday Tuesday

Wednesday Thursday Friday

Saturday Sunday

My favourite day is

Bingo

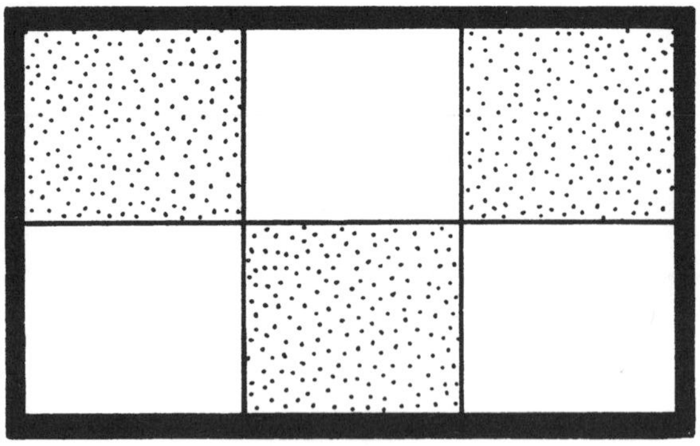

Game 1

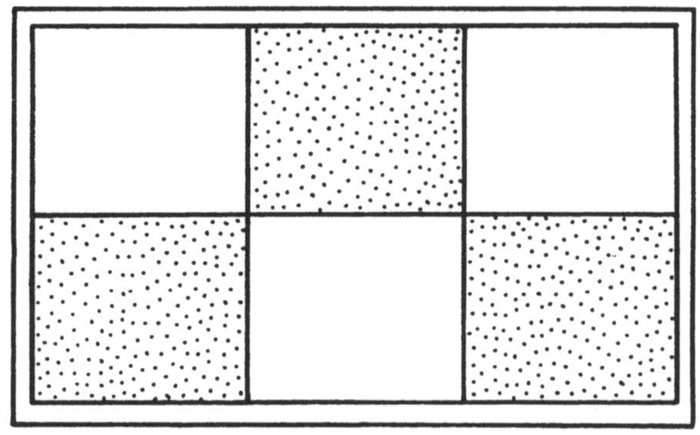

Game 2

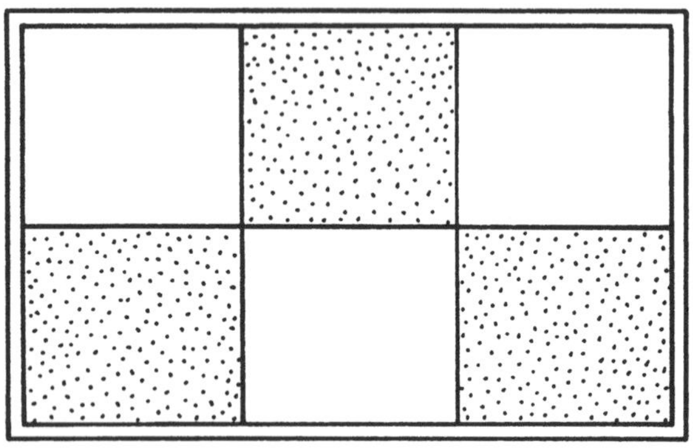

Game 3

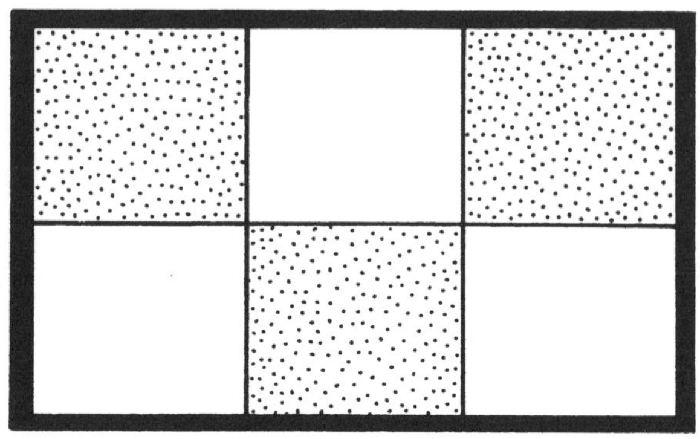

Game 4

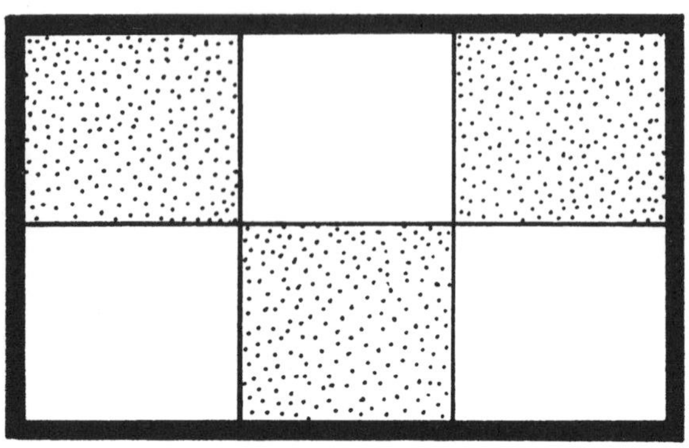

Game 5

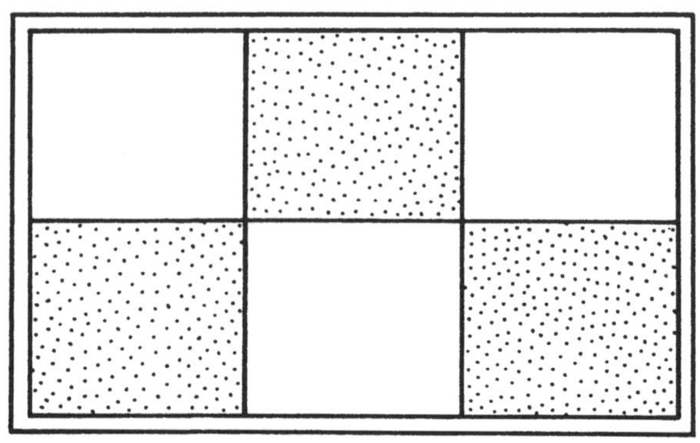

Game 6

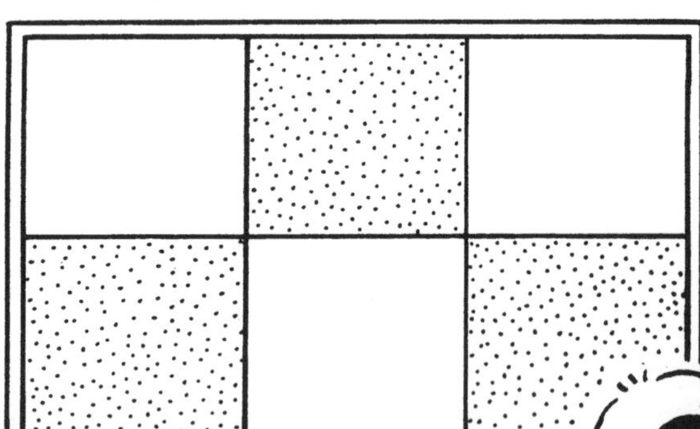

Game 7

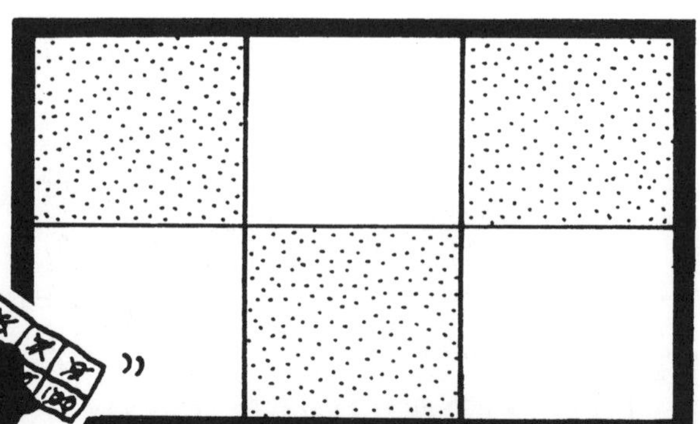

Game 8

532197
823575
243365
1

2

64
66
68
Lemon Street
3

CHOCOLATE
Coke
4

29
25
5

11:45
6

Bikes

TIM'S BIKE

saddle

back brake

back light

back reflector

bell

front brake

front light

front reflector

POLLY'S BIKE

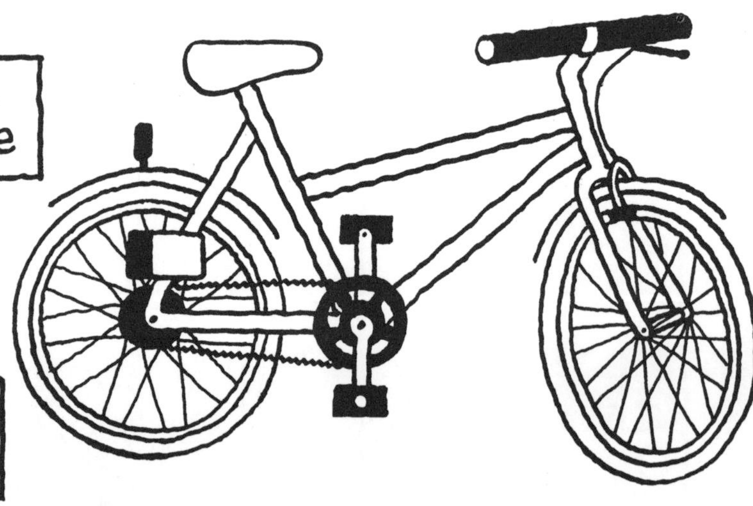

saddle

back brake

back light

back reflector

bell

front brake

front light

front reflector

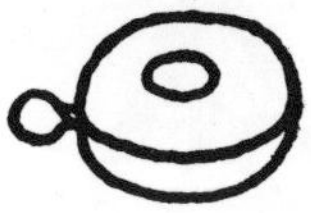

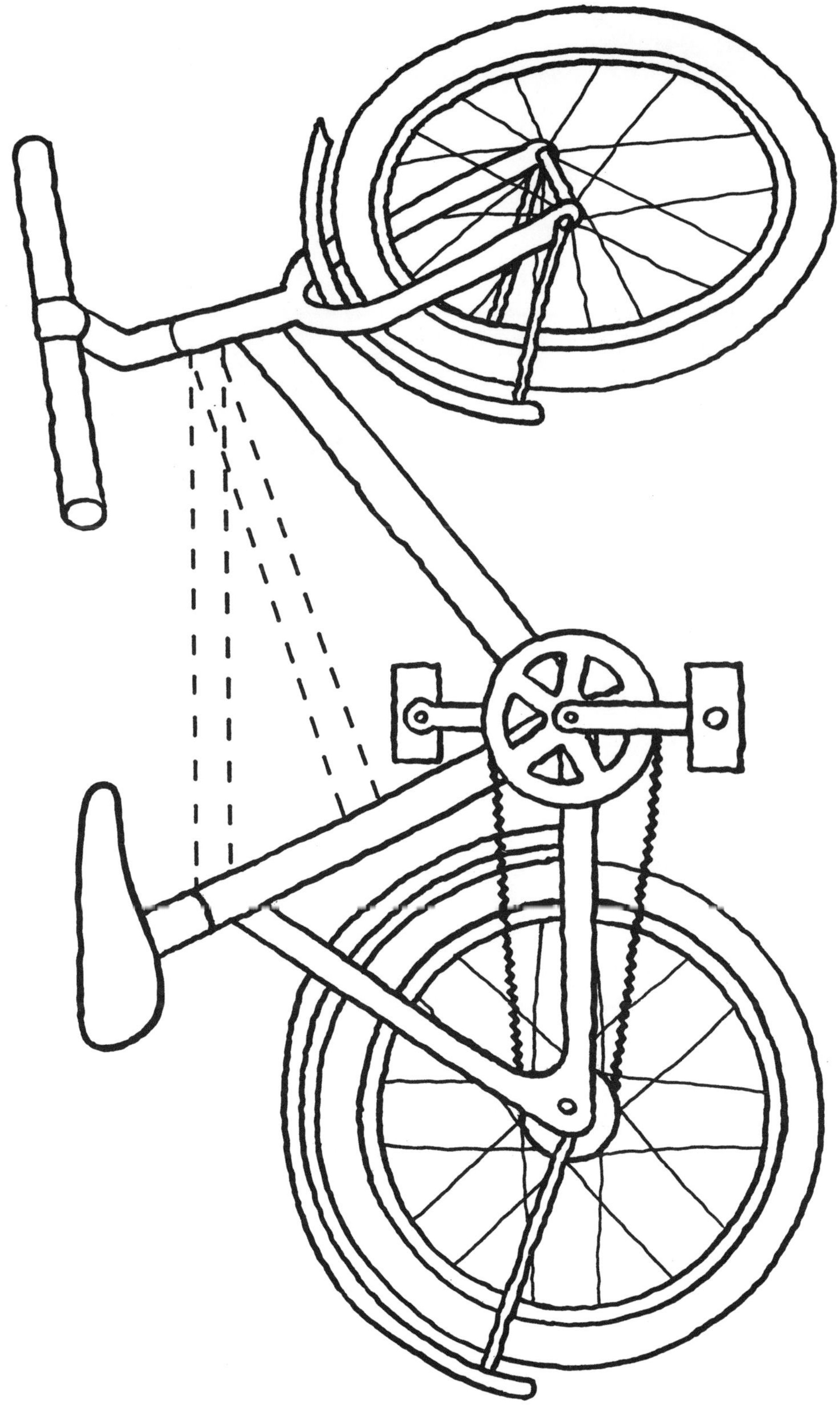

8 Traffic signs

(1) turn right here

(2) turn left here

(3) go straight on

(4) wait

(5) walk

(6) stop

Grandma's accident

10

The family photos

1. ______________________

2. ______________________

3. ______________________

4. ______________________
____
____
____

5. ______________________
____

aunty uncle father mother
cousins grandma grandpa

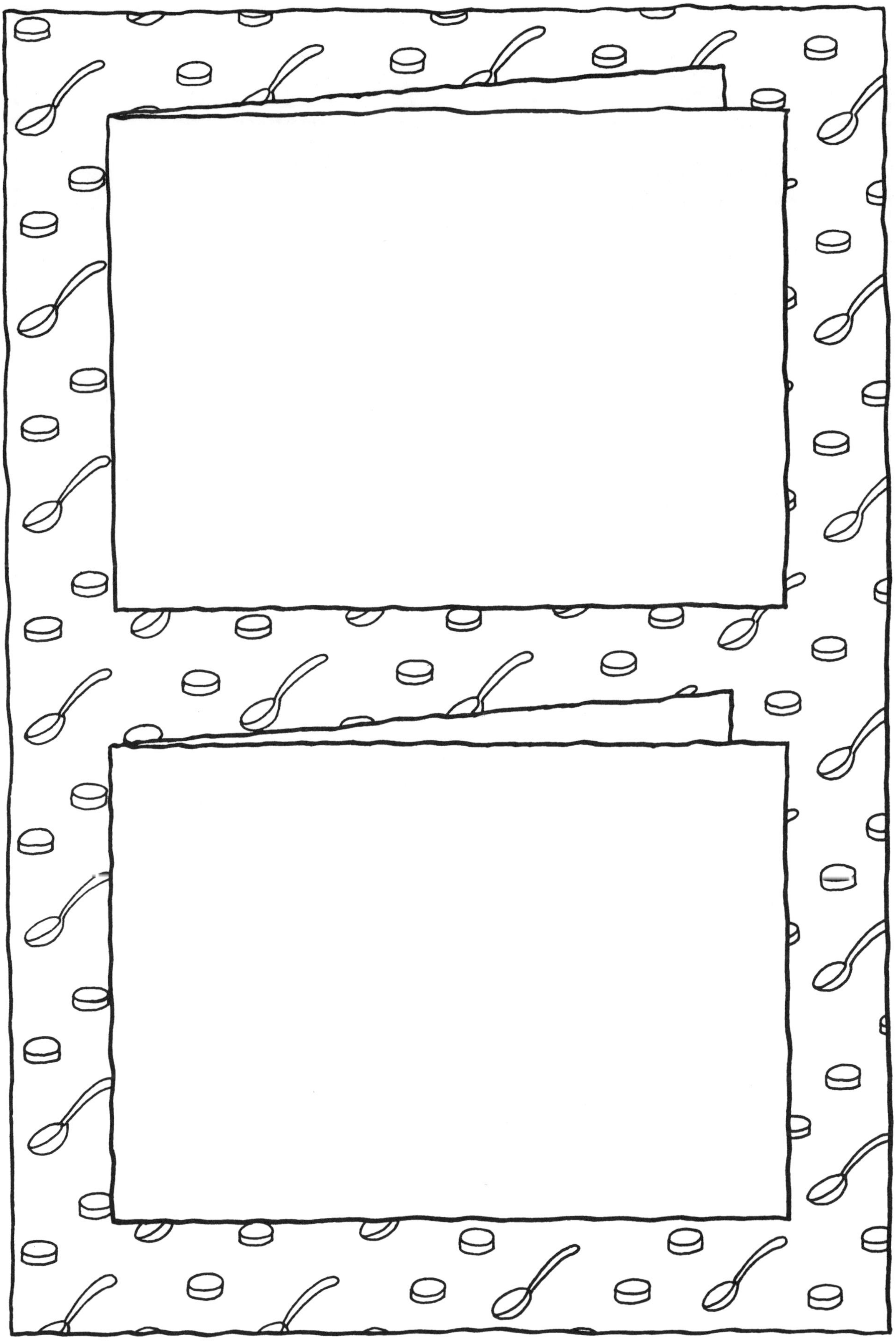

12

What's the matter with … ?

Name:

a broken leg	
a tummy ache	
a cold	

Name:

a broken leg	
a tummy ache	
a cold	

Name:

a broken leg	
a tummy ache	
a cold	

Name:

a broken leg	
a tummy ache	
a cold	

Blackie Tigger Harry Princess

14 Kooky and the doctor

16

Christmas cards

Ben
Mark
Little Red Hen
DOG
BISCUITS

The Snow Princess

M__ch

Ap___

M_y

season:

J__e

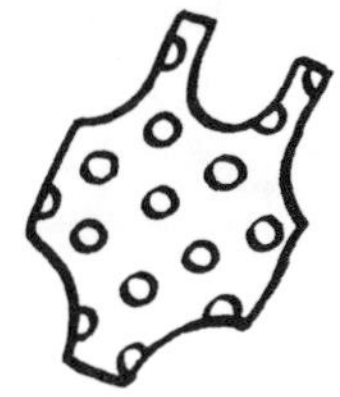

J__y

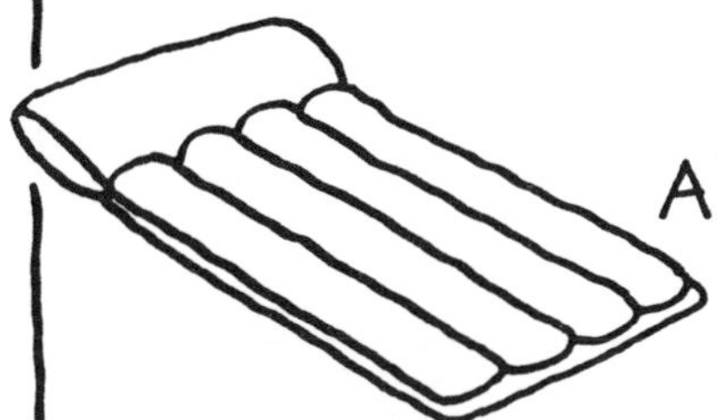

A_g__t

season:

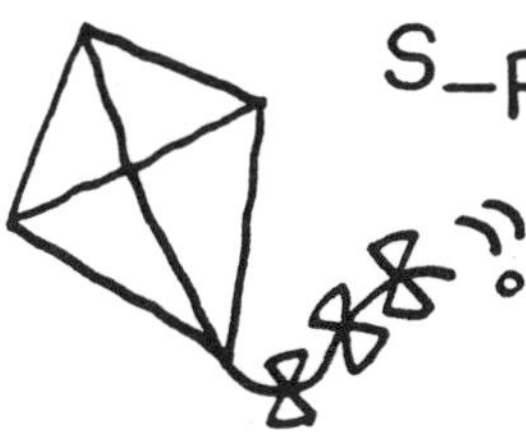

S_pt___er

Oc__b__

N_v____r

season:

D_c__ber

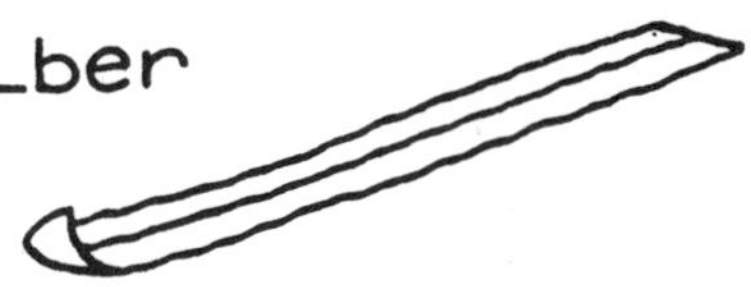

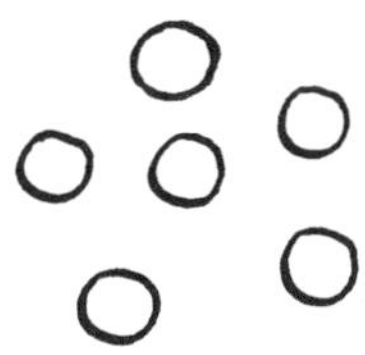

Ja_ua__

Fe_r__ry

season:

winter spring summer autumn

20 Winter things

◯ sledge	◯ ski suit	◯ woolly hat
◯ skis	◯ headband	◯ ski pants
◯ anorak	◯ scarf	◯ gloves
◯ skates	◯ pullover	◯ boots

Tom's woolly hat:	
	It's too big.
	It fits.

Tom's anorak:	
	It's too small.
	It's too long.

Tom's ski pants:	
	They're too big.
	They're too short.

Amy's pullover:	
	It's too long.
	It's too short.

Amy's skirt:	
	It fits.
	It's too long.

Amy's socks:	
	They're too long.
	They're too short.

22

Let's go skating

Kooky and his □□□□□□

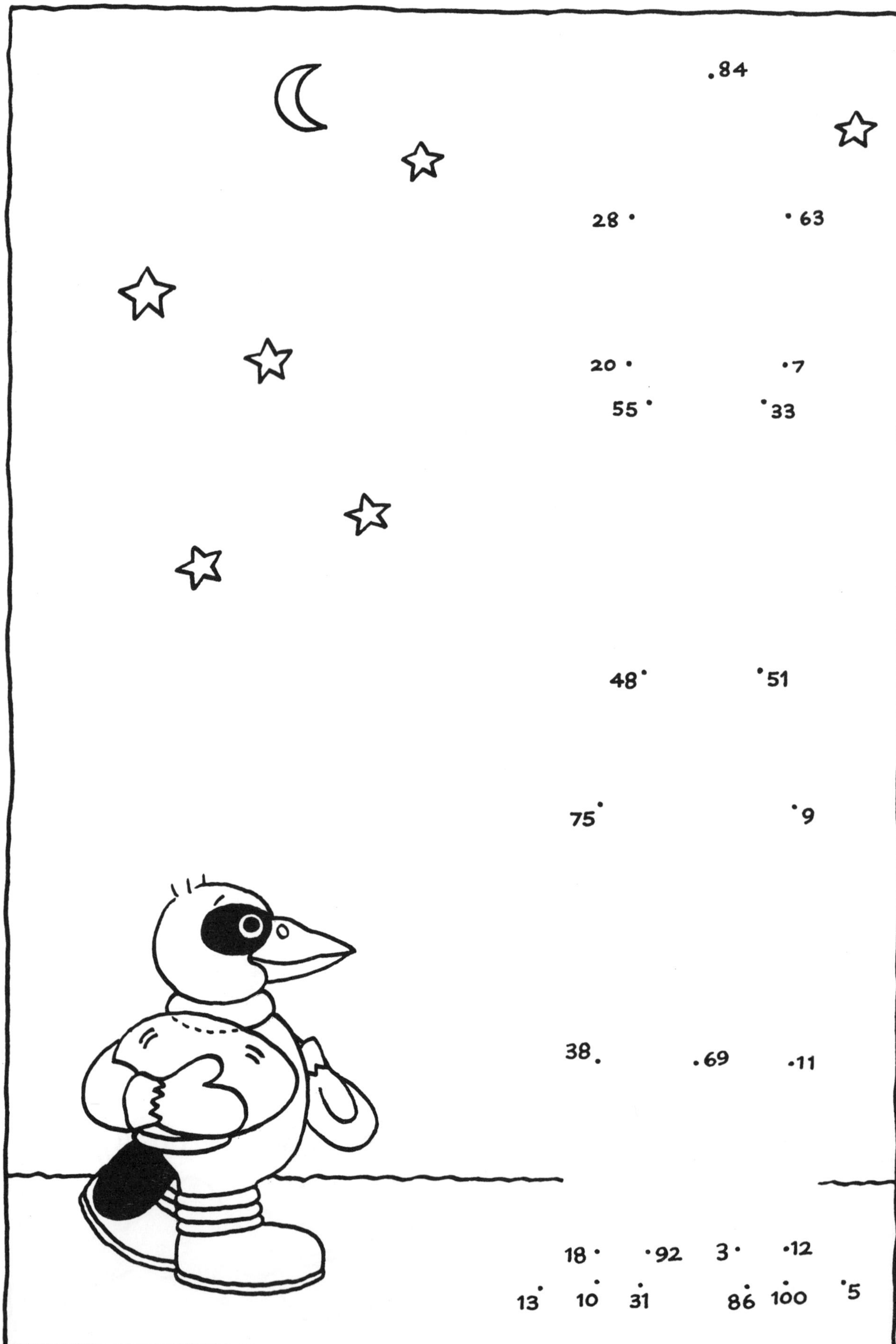

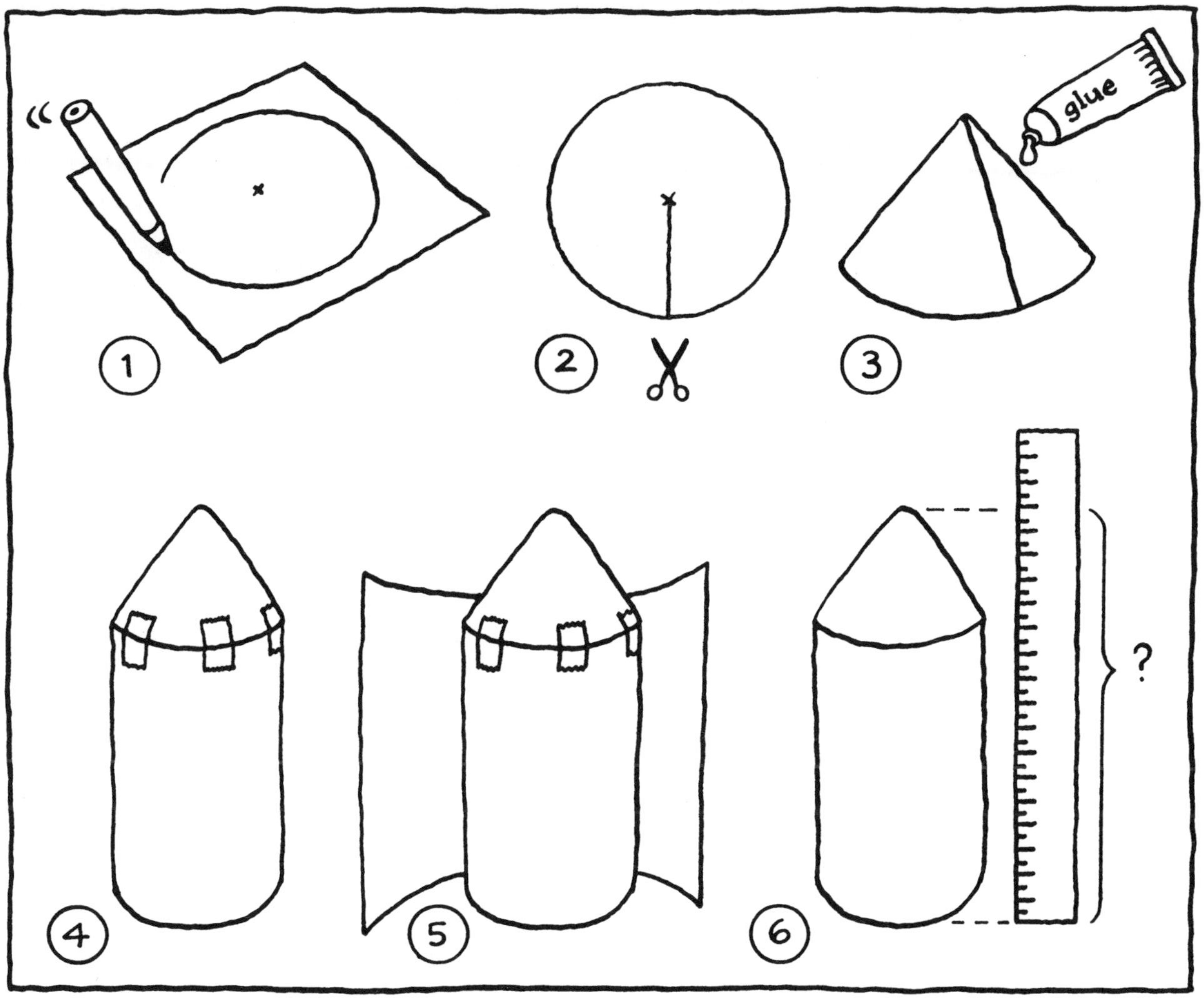

My rocket is

____
(colours)

It's _____ cm long.

26 Meeting on the moon

Gamma

Alpha

Kooky

Delta

Beta

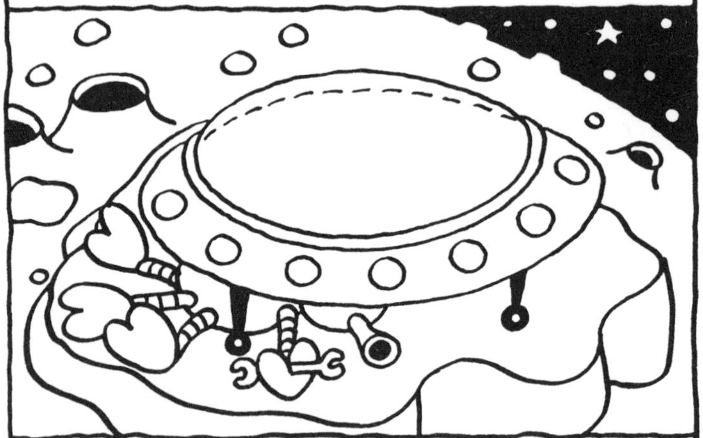

in

on

under

next to

in front of

behind

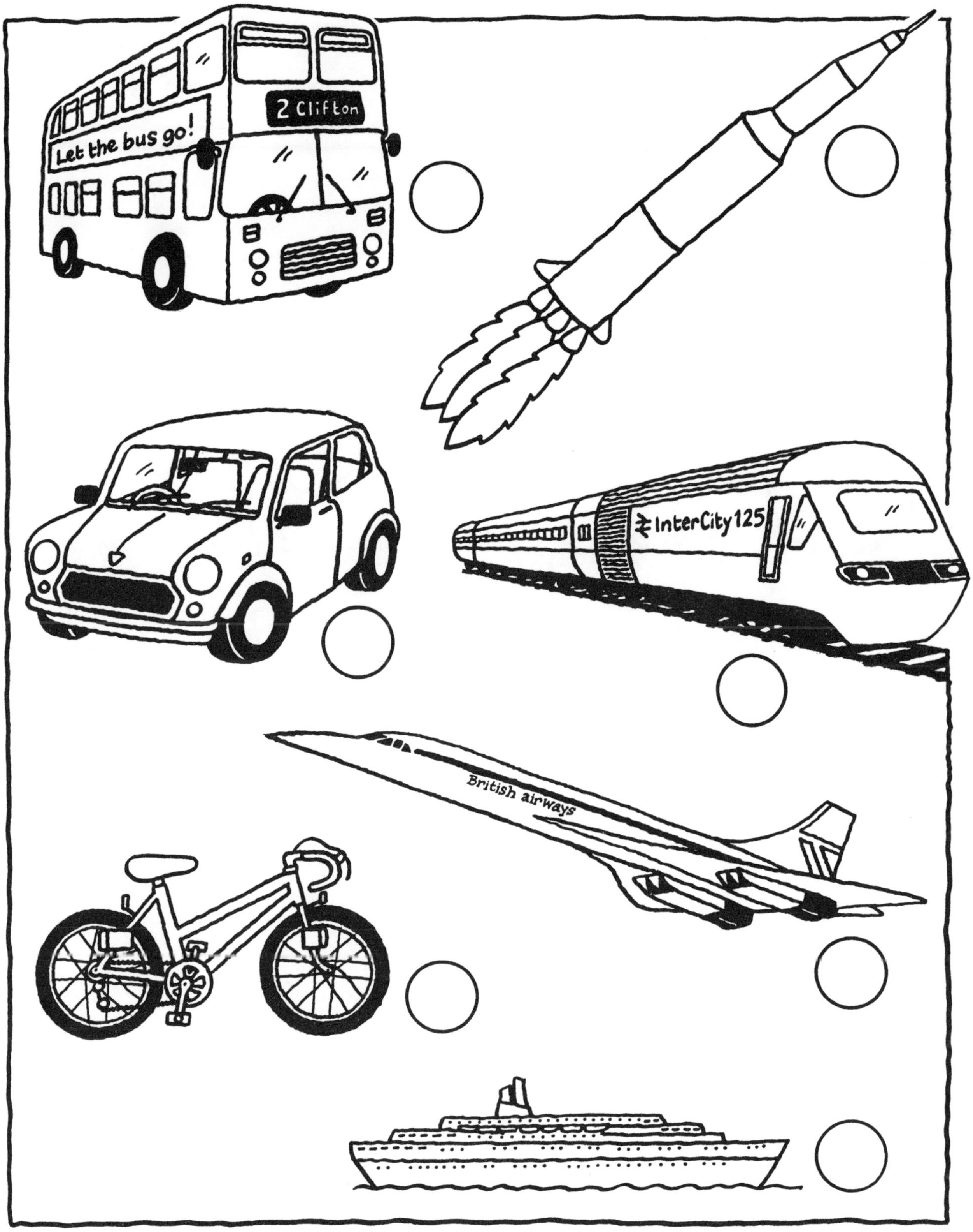

bus bike train ship

plane rocket car

Postcards

My postcard is from:

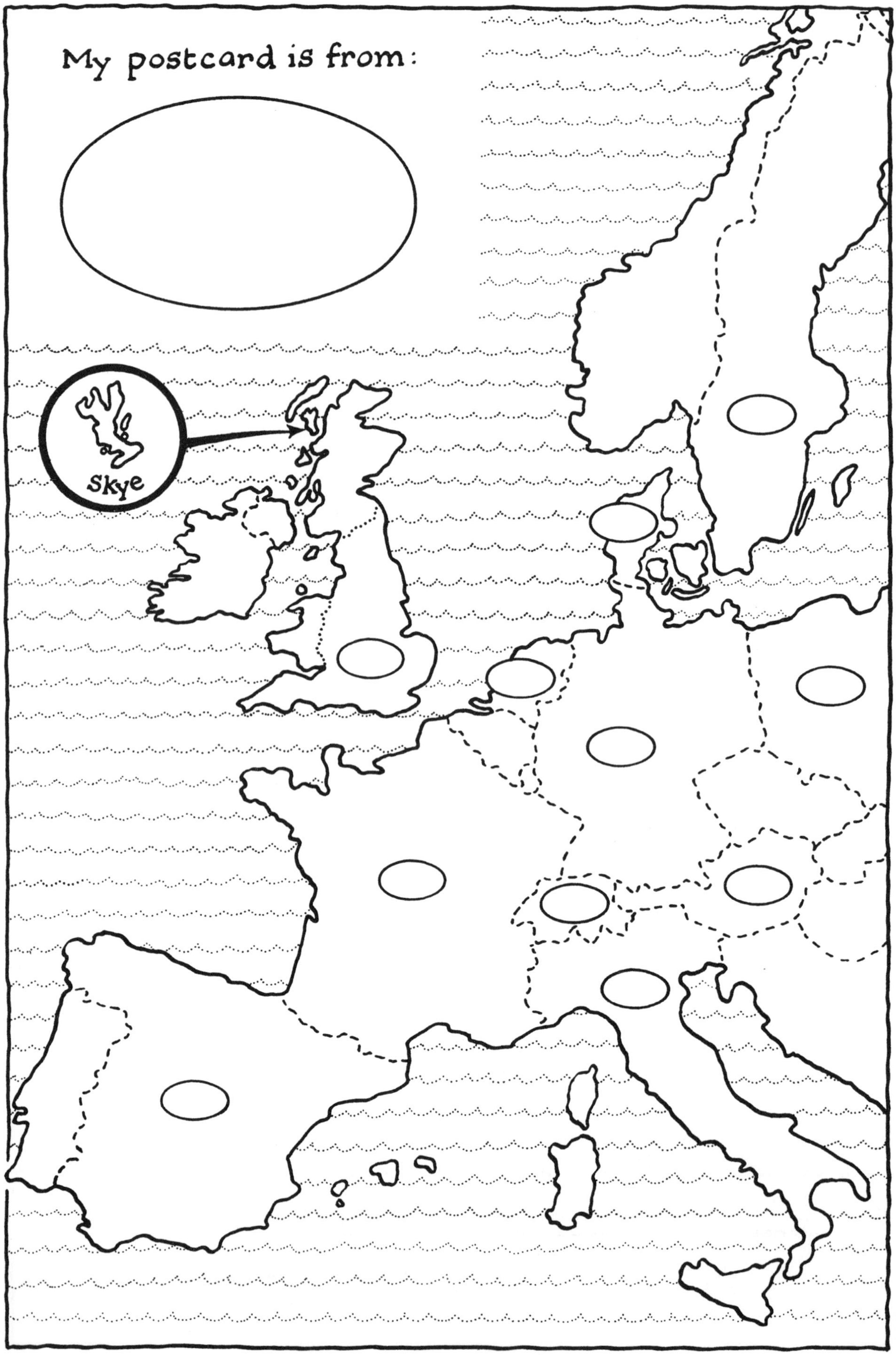

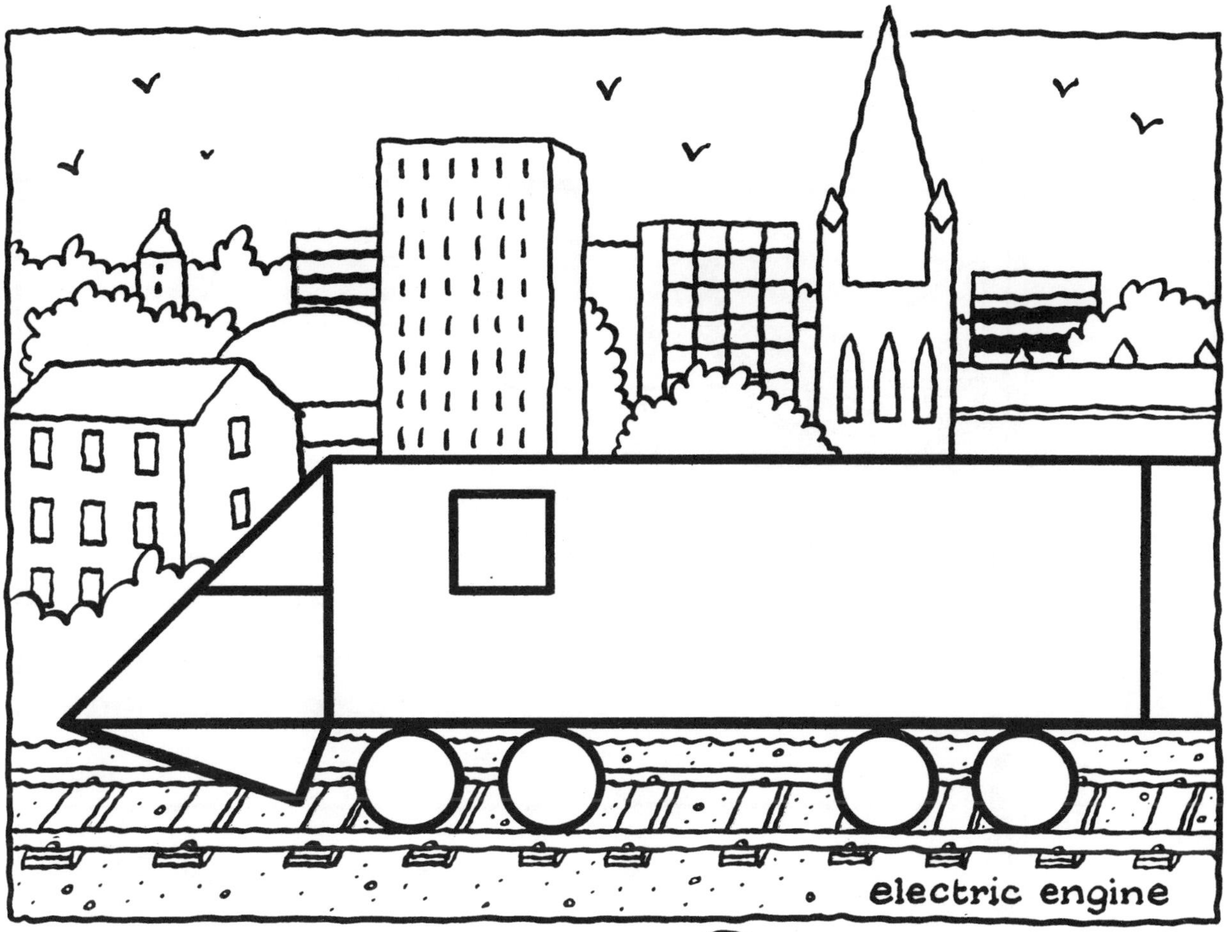
electric engine

steam engine

Old and new trains

1 Top speed: ______ km/h

1829

2 Top speed: ______ km/h

1835

3 Top speed: ______ km/h

1991

Sowing seeds

The caterpillar game

34 Jenny's flowerbed

Let's look for the Easter eggs

Jenny and Mark's stall

Renting bikes

The Jacksons on the way to Skye

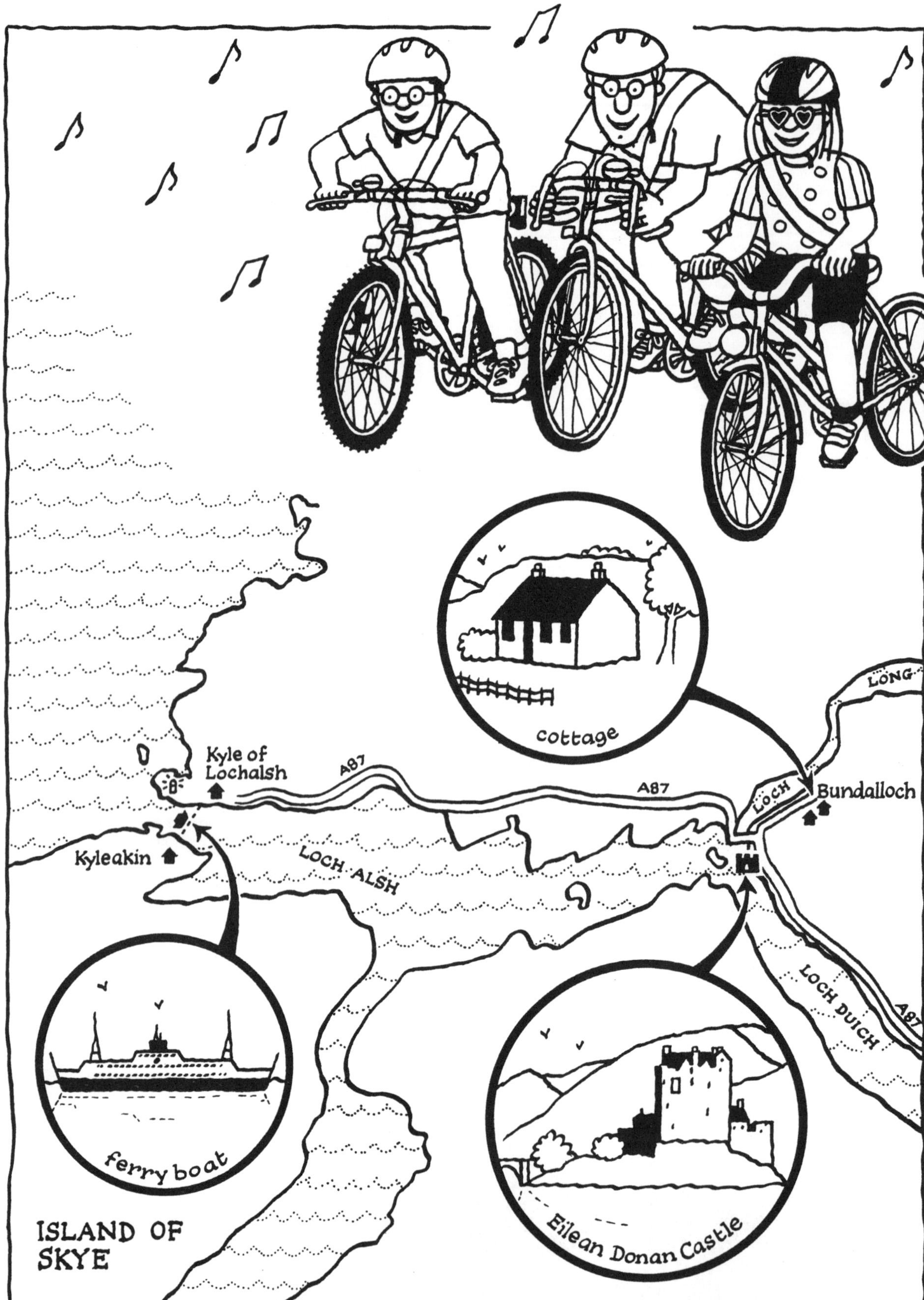

When I'm old, you can have my treasure.
Let's play: The ghost of the castle.
My favourite game.
I love my castle.
Where's the treasure?
I don't know.
Here's a gold coin and a silver coin.
Thank you, King.
Sun 7 January
Oh, the poor King.

Where's the treasure?

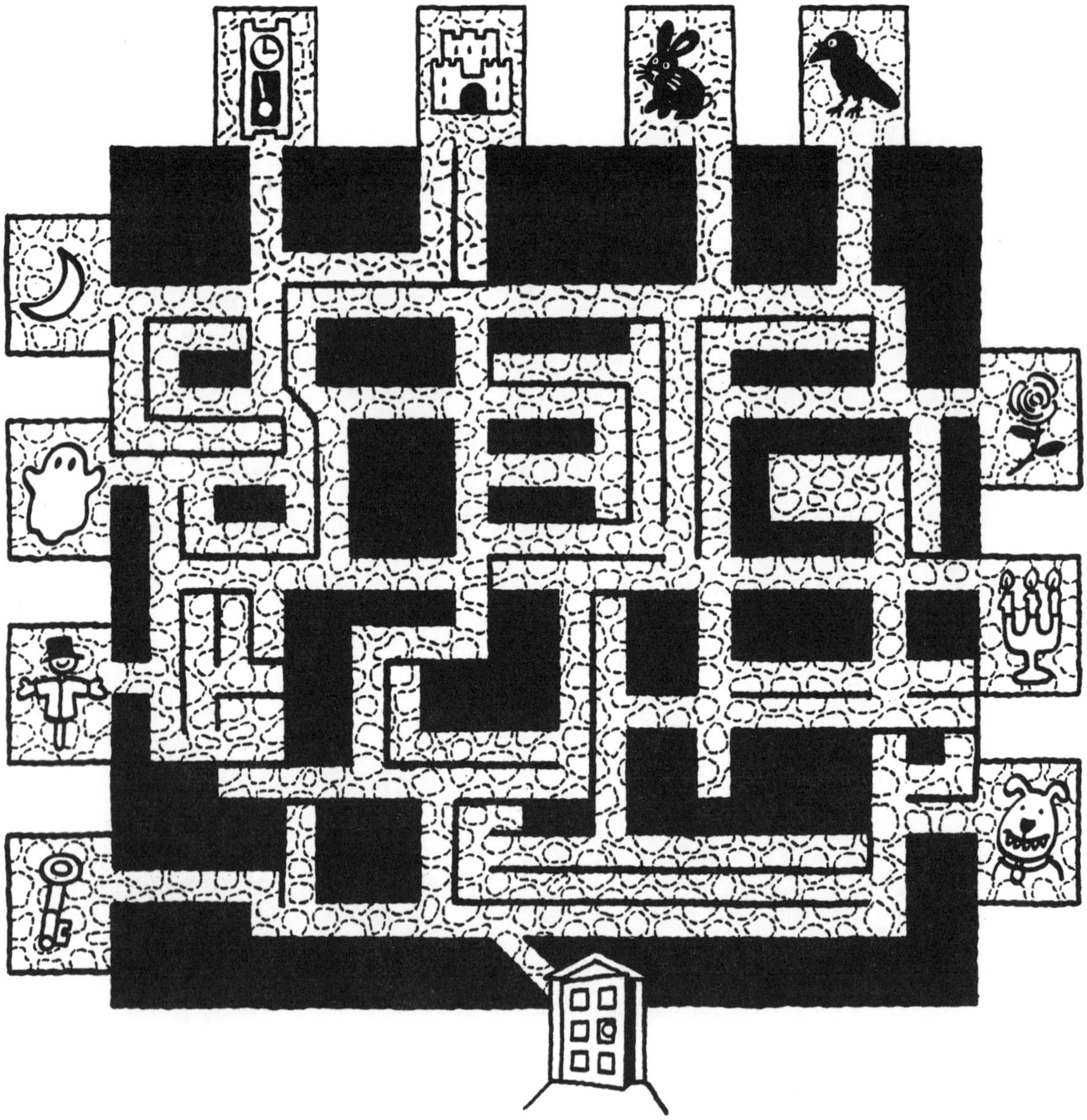

The treasure is in the room with the ____________

	clock		key		black bird
	moon		dog		rabbit
	ghost		candles		castle
	scarecrow		flower		

I've got ______ trousers and a ______ hat,
My nose is ______, just look at that!
______ is my mouth and ______ is my face,
My shoes are the biggest in this place.
With my ______ jacket and my funny ______ hair,
Come to the circus, you'll find me there.

Tumble Ted Bobo

Jacko Coco Ned

CIRCUS
SARAGASSI
Monday
Tuesday
Wednesday
Thursday
Friday
Saturday
Sunday
TICKETS: £ £ £
Family ticket: £

Mr Magic

elephant
tiger
pigeon
snake
kookaburra
lamb
dog
mouse
cat
cow
duck
donkey
pig

46

Read and write

T 1

swimming | riding a bike | football

Philip's hobby is ____________________.

My hobby is ____________________.

T 2

clean | dirty | new | old

Philip's bike is ________ and ____________.

My (dream) bike is __________ and ________.

T 3

turn left | turn right | stop | walk

Here's the traffic sign for ______________.

The red traffic sign is for ______________.

T 4

uncle | aunty | cousin | brother

Mark's ________________ is in Australia.

My __________ is in ______________.

T 5

a broken arm | a broken leg | a cold

Princess has got ____________________.

I haven't got ____________________.

T 6

an orange | medicine | soap

Kooky has got ______________ for his cough.

I've got ____________ for my __________.

Read and write

T 7

sheep	cow	donkey	dog

The ______________ isn't in the crib.

The ________ and the ________ are in the crib.

T 8

biscuit	recorder	stocking

Ben has got a ________ in his ____________.

Can I have a ________ in my ____________?

T 9

spring	summer	autumn	winter

January is in ______________________.

My birthday is in ______________________.

T 10

pullover	scarf	anorak	woolly hat

Tom's ______________________ is too long.

My ______________ is too ______________.

T 11

plane	rocket	flying saucer	bike

Beta has got a ______________________.

My friend has got a ______________________.

T 12

by bus	by car	by bike	on foot

Jenny goes to school ______________________.

I go to ______________________.

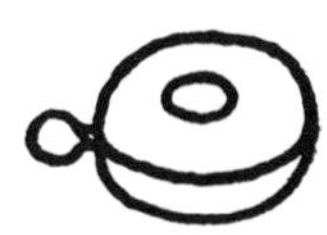

48 Read and write

T 13

Germany Britain Holland Austria

The teacher's postcard is from ______________.

My ______________ is from ______________.

T 14

carrots beans peas flowers

Kooky hasn't got ______________ in his garden.

I like ______________ and ______________.

T 15

caterpillar butterfly flower

Kooky has got a ______________ in his garden.

My favourite ______________ is ______________.

T 16

skylark scarecrow farmer birds

The ____________ has got four baby ____________.

I like the ______________________________ best.

Kooky
Unterrichtswerk für den frühbeginnenden Englischunterricht
Activity Book 2

Im Auftrage des Verlages herausgegeben und erarbeitet von: Leonora Fröhlich-Ward, München · Ludwig Waas, München · Angelika Hillen, München · Hannelies Stellwag, Riedering

Verlagsredaktion: Marie Keenoy, Ursula Fuchs

Beratende Mitwirkung: Ingrid Behnken, Vaterstetten · Manfred Ehringer, Stuttgart · Ingrid Fechner, Kassel · Helga Friederix, Habichtswald · Rita Heil, Edenkoben · Christiane Lücke, Telgte · Susanne von der Schulenburg, Bonn · Wolfgang Soldan, Brownsville, Texas *sowie* Prof. Peter Doyé, Braunschweig · Prof. Dr. Peter W. Kahl, Hamburg

Grafik: Frances Cony, Bristol, England
Technische Umsetzung: Matthias Fuchs

1. Auflage – 2. Druck 1994
Alle Drucke dieser Auflage können, weil untereinander unverändert, im Unterricht nebeneinander verwendet werden.

Druck: Druckhaus Langenscheidt, Berlin

ISBN 3-464-00143 -1
Bestellnummer 1431